32 twisted turns

32 twisted turns

Anna Schmalinsky

NEW ACADEMIA PUBLISHING · SCARITH

Washington, DC

Library of Congress Control Number: 2020919145
ISBN 978-1-7348659-9-8 (alk. paper)

 An imprint of New Academia Publishing

 New Academia Publishing
4401-A Connecticut Avenue NW #236, Washington DC 20008
info@newacademia.com - www.newacademia.com

Contents

From the Author

For me writing was always a way out–something I could always rely on. When the words stream right from your heart. But what is even more important, is when these words are read. This is why I have decided to publish my first experiences of writing in English, although it is a lot harder for me than writing in Russian, because these two languages are way too different in almost everything. Nevertheless, I am very happy to present to you, my readers, these 32 twisted turns of my thoughts.

Anna Schmalinsky

1. Things that I like

I don't like writing
It makes me feel exposed, open and readable
It makes me a victim of my own words
And it sucks
Because I write not only for myself
But also for the readers
And yet I don't want to be read
And yet I am

I don't like talking about myself
I need it
I really do
But I don't like it for the very same reason
Because trusting yourself either to your friends or to your readers
Sucks pretty much anyway
Now you don't know them – but you made sure they know you

I don't like monologues
When the words clutter up my cerebral activity
I find myself unable to stop them
They curl up in a big rotting flock of hair
And I have to cough them out
In order to keep breathing

I don't like compassion
Because when I am in sorrow
I need it
And it makes me feel vulnerable
Because I want to be pet on my head
Given a sweet treat

And told that everything will be ok
Although we all know that it won't

I don't like being loved
Even more than loving somebody myself
Because when somebody truly needs you
In every way that is possible
And wants you to be more than just being your own
It is frustrating
And it feels scary
And unknown
And new
And
I hate it

2. I am not an actress

An act is something that we do
In order to trick each other
Or ourselves

The evolution of a famous actress – of a star
Takes too many stages and unfortunately there is only 33.3 percent
    chance of becoming successful
And 66.6 other chances are to become a real nobody or even less
    than that
We act
To trick the whole IAMHAPPY universe
And become a real White Dwarf
Or just an ordinary neutron star

Or a bLACK hOLE
Because when we fail –
We suck everybody in to go down together
And so we act
We take these chances

3. The never-read poem

When I look at you the problem is that I don't see enough
The dim light of my bedroom makes your face blurry, leaves it
    unnoticed
And those parts of you which are in the circle of light–I don't
    want to see

Sometimes I wonder why I am with you
Although I know you were the best option for me at that time
But now I am not so sure
For some reason I am not

I was never sure about you
Even when you were right by my side
Your cold hands sliding through me
Leaving nothing behind but just emptiness
And when your fresh mint breath slightly touched my nose
I wanted nothing but to feel it on my heart
And for some reason I didn't

Of course distance makes it harder
 Makes me think about you only in the morning and in the
    evening
Sometimes at around three or four pm
But never more than that
Never

I answer when you text me, sometimes I text first just to check
    that I am still needed
I ask our friends if you are still waiting for me
But the problem is not you

It never was
Probably not even me
It's Us

And so I keep wondering why I can't go away
Why every time when I go out of the plane I look for your
    face in the crowd of smiles
Although I hardly remember how exactly you look like
And I still want you to love me
But I don't want to love you back
I never did

I know what you will think when you read this
You will say I played you
But maybe we were both played
You never got the love you deserved
And I never got to love you back

So let these words stay unnoticed
Just like so many other unnoticed things between us
When the time is right I will go away
I promise

Because what I really want is for us to die not with each
other

With somebody else

4. Thirteen ways of looking at your corpse

My hands shaking
In blunt honesty of the moment
You are lying in front of me with a bullet in your love
If you were actually dead
It would be easier
But right now there is only me and the smell of your death
in my nostrils

The flowers on my table
Are still fresh and still alive
Are you?
I've colored my hair and I've colored
My sentiments in black
Since we last met. Now they match the color of your skin.

When I kiss you goodbye
You let your smile become a memory
Although I know exactly why I will meet you in hell
Because my cancer wouldn't stop in front of God

I sit by your side in the morning
And you sing me the song your mother used to sing you
When you couldn't sleep
But right now I am falling to the kingdom of Morpheus
And your death cannot stop me from that

A cup on my night table
Is empty
It was full yesterday when you were dying on my arms
And now the one who is empty is you

And when I laugh at your weird hairstyle
The priest looks at me as if I had a demon hiding inside
But I cannot stop because they are all so funny
And my today is funny as well

I've decided to keep your in an urn
Close to my bed
So I could see you in my dreams
But I don't dream
And you are dead of course

You were always the guardian of my household
You watered my dried heart
And wiped my dusty hands
Even when I was sick and couldn't say «thank you»
You brought me a glass of red wine
Even though my lips were closed

I stand by your side
And feel your warm breath on my cheekbones
Your smile choking me, squeezing my lungs
Leaving red marks all over my ribs
It hurts even now

Although I have decided to write this poem about you
The words get stuck in my fingers
As I print them on your old computer
Wiping off your fingerprints
And leaving my own instead

8

When I had my first chemotherapy
I threw up on your shirt
And you threw up all my love

And tomorrow I am having my last procedure
The first and the last one with your dead corpse
On my arms
And the smell of your death in my nostrils

Inspired by Wallace Stevens' «Thirteen Ways of Looking at a Blackbird»

5. I will tear you apart on my own, so you will stop breathing, having convulsions lying in my arms. I will bury you next to my old house, without any memorial, without a "happy" photograph, with no flowers. I will bury you on my own. Leaving your beating heart in my jewelery box.

I will tear you apart on my own
Rip off every single bone inside
Reach your heart, reach your dead empty soul
Just like you it was never alive

Just like you I've been wanting to die
Not alone, God, but maybe with you
Be reborn, be like you. No? Revive
My desire in your dirty bones.

Hit me once, hit me twice. No? But why?
Don't be gentle, I do not deserve
Be devoured untouched by your love
Just destroy my own little «inside»

Let me cry, let me love, not be loved
Let me steal, not be caught, but forgiven
Let me be far away from your side
Let me die next to you. Let me. Please

Break my nose so I cannot breathe
Step on my face with your ego
Beat me to death, but revive
My desire in your dirty bones

6. Dedicated to my dear no one

I've always liked the idea of caring less
Caring less about everything with an exception of my studies
    and university. Maybe.

I think I have reached my minimum of giving a shit this
    summer after the quarantine
during which I have experienced a couple of troublesome
    nervous breakdowns (I am still not sure if that's
exactly what you can call my previous state), maybe mild
    anxiety based on trying to quit smoking, and in June I
had my very first panic attack.
So here I am now and I honestly don't care

In the past six months I can say I've seen enough
I've seen my mom crying more than I thought I would ever
    see in my whole entire life
I've also picked up more empty beers in my house than it is
    appropriate
I've seen so many pills left on the dinner table, that I actually
    had an idea of taking them all myself
And guess what
I didn't go deeper into myself and I still don't want to think
    that maybe my family has some issues, or maybe it
is even me who has them
Or maybe the whole planet Earth has them too
I don't care tbh

And that's one of the reasons people of my age find me very
    adult, because I prefer going with the flow, going
with a feeling

Meaning that I generally do what I want
And although I end up drinking at least 4 days in a week and smok-
    ing so many juul pods that I have nowhere to
keep them anymore
I am enjoying this summer
I admit that I might scare some of my friends a bit, because some of
    my stories seem to be a bit too much to be
told, although they are never about me directly
And I look way too easygoing for them, I behave the way I want,
    saying what I want, doing what I want

Some of the girls envy me, some of the guys sympathize with me,
    admire me even
But I prefer closing my eyes when I don't want to see or to be seen

Of course you, my dear reader, might think that I will end up
    becoming a junky, a drug dealer or a drug addict,
or all of the above
Well and who knows, but I doubt it
You might also think that I don't care about my life at all
And this is completely not true
I am just nice to people I like, a bitch to people who irritate me,
    lovely to my boyfriend and understanding to
most of the people, so they usually say that I even care too much
    about everything haha
But the problem is they are also wrong just the way you are, honey
I am able to choose
And yet I am completely unable to understand where the real me is
    among all these mirror reflections

7. ***

Life is a mess–they said.
Life is full of surprises–they repeated again and again.
But I looked up to the cloudless forever sleepless sky and
    wondered–
Is it actually that hard to predict what's next?
Aren't we the ones who put the comma or the question mark??
Didn't I make each of those mistakes consciously not letting life
    put a period?

Now when my friend calls and tells me she was raped when she
took a half of ecstasy pill
Do I not blame myself for not paying more attention to her
    because I saw this coming but I didn't give a damn?
And when she tells me her new boyfriend was or still is addicted
    to meph why do I say nothing?
I don't give a shit but do I do this because I choose so or because
    I cannot do otherwise?
Because when she goes lower and lower with each step literally
    falling apart I am too busy with my own life to even try to
    help.
Or maybe this is just an excuse.
I say to myself I am tired and nothing can be done here.
And I am sure I choose to do so.
So is it a surprise that she will end up like my other ex-suicid-
    al-friend?
Because I wouldn't be actually surprised.
Because when this girl with always covered hands turns up on
    my front door completely losing her shit not even being able
    to stand properly I don't open the door.
I don't open the door because I am with my boyfriend.
And so they both are my fault at the end, because
    I AM TOO FUCKING BUSY

8. DIY

he slept on clouds
And occasionally when he stepped down I could hold his
    hand and say: "it will be ok"
He always nodded in agreement
But I saw the moon in his eyes

I always talked for about an hour or two
And then stepped out of the coffin
Of the cubicle
Of the hospital itself
Because if I stayed one more second it would engulf my hope

And it did one day

He used to be a child
But I looked at him then and saw just a crew of catheters and
    sheets pulled up to his chin
Just a little mess of depression, anxiety and Xanax
And me sitting next to his bed, trying to tie his hopes together

And now I am sitting ALONE trying to tie MY hopes together
Because when I realized I had failed my knitting of his soul
I had to rip him away from my heart
And I am stuck with nothing to make a patch

9. In the world's flat

I'm looking for the fifth corner
In a room fool of empty chairs
I hear the swearing of a squeaky doorbell
I've lost the door itself. So many stairs
Around me keep turning left and right
To take me out or to lure me into darkness
Or maybe it's the lightbulb of my empty flat
She's hanging down desperately in a choking cuddle

I step aside from now on
Let the walls come closer to my toes
And let them brake into my little inner world
The flat is left
The stairs are still
The person's knocking gave up into madness

10. ***

He said "no"
And this word cut through me
Turned my thoughts inside out
And left them breathlessly suffocating
In my uncorked empty heart

It shook me like a bottle of Fanta
And frightened, my soul was bubbling–
Creating the enormous pressure inside

And so I burst.

Sometimes I hope a splinter cut him in half
Sometimes I hope it only left a little scratch
On his white, silver fish-like skin
But of course it couldn't

Not because I loved him, I surely did not
But because he didn't love even the beautiful illusion of me
Which I created FOR him

He used to say I was boring
I was, but I was also petrified by him
By what I let him do
By what I didn't

And maybe if his sad dog-eyes did not remind me of a wolf
And if his kisses did not remind me of a soul reaper
I would make myself be his princess
Although he is not a prince, neither a knight
Not even a dragon

He is like a water droplet
In which you can see yourself for just a second
And when it cracks open on the ground
There is nothing left but a memory

Or nothing left at all

And so he did not say "yes"

11. Autumn days

Recently days are fox-colored
Sneaking through my life trying to stay in shade
Howling, crying, making sounds which I cannot comprehend
I screw my eyes and still the reality is cutting through my
    shrunken pupils
I am fox-colored. Not red.

My naked feet are noiseless, my sense of smell is disgusted by
    stinking weeks
Flying by and never coming back
I go down the stairs of my callous routine
There is no trace to be followed–I cannot come up again
And the world devours me with fox-colored teeth

I've lost my sense of self-preservation, I've lost my fur
My skin is blue, I am cold and yet I cuddle myself with my
    rat-tail
It used to be fox-colored too
If I die no fox-body will be left
Days will become rat-colored and my rat-corpse will rot forever
    on the steps of reality

12. 420 sec

Seven minutes ago I needed to start
Crying.
Seven hours ago I still couldn't say
A word.
Seven beautiful days. I wasn't sure
In dying.
Seven terrible months. I needed to make it
Stop.

Alone or together with my little-enough-
Thought.
Creating weather conditions for my
Own end.
A spoon or a knife. Maybe rope. Smoke a dope–
All for naught.
The sign on the road told me to make a
Stop.

And now I am waiting for never-sleeping
Patrol.
Waiting-night-gazing–stargazing into the
Light.
Trying to smoke but I don't have a Light-
-Er.
Ashes on my naked knees could't help it but
Stop.   Existing.

Surely not. Surely maybe I Am
Sick.
My mind trying to leave me one nuisance

Quits.
I'm looking at freezing icicles. I'm scared to
Lick.
Maybe my tongue will forget every kiss. I
Stop.

Stop believing, stop praying, stop stopping
Again.
Stop breathing, stop holding my breath under-
Life.
Stop living, stop loving, stop laughing. I will forget and
Stop.
And Stop. Now Stop. Don't Stop. Last Stop. Last thought and
I Stop.

13. Silent life

My life wants to talk
and I am not ready
—Chalk

Is black on my soul
I can't swipe it off
—Memories

merging with silky reality
Each of them rhymes with little sick laugh

Is someone here
        Or are we alone
                Am I sincere
                    Or honesty's gone

Talking to mirrors of your silent life
I cannot help it but choose to be deaf
As
—Blindness wouldn't do any good
The noise of your
—life will always be rude

14. Sick people

Give me a pill, a vaccine, a shot
Something to cease my realism
I see you becoming endlessly old
I see us becoming younger together

Sooner or later the blood supply stops
Each memory's left hanging to bleed
And we. We are looking at Us from beneath
A life, A routine, A love. This last beat
Of our heart is bringing us closer
At the end of the tunnel there is a monster

Or should I call it the light?
Maybe none of it's right

15. YOU LOST. WANT TO PLAY AGAIN?

I thought I lost myself when
I was losing tears
I thought I lost myself when I was eating bread with salt
When my sandcastle was around nine years old
I thought I lost myself completely
And at the age of nine and a couple teardrops
It was washed off by my abandoned mother

I thought I lost myself when
I was a little older
When I was putting more suncream on my
Still almost young not-face
I thought I lost myself when I was driving way too fast
Along the Red Square
And I lost myself again

I almost lost myself that time
Although my absence wasn't a surprise
To my dead classmates and my father
Who was raised up in a communal grave
I thought I lost myself when
My not-yet-too-big-boobs were way too small for bras
And then I lost myself when my mother said not to laugh
About her different socks

I thought I lost myself when
I believed I didn't
And I as well believed my tea was like not-coffee
But with sugar and with salt
Or sweets Or sweat Or sweater
I had a sweater? Was it Cold?

I thought I lost myself when
They all said I lost my mind

16. Hey mom

When I was young, around eight or nine
I used to feel I was a very special girl
I thought I was the center of attention
The center of the whole universe
I used to dream how I would find love,
Not only in someone, but also in myself
How I would be successful and the most
Amazing girl among the rest

And soon when I turned 12 I thought I found love
You know, that very childish type
When you're afraid to take his hand
But yet you both believe you're a couple
And when your dreams are finally above
The Sun, above the Moon, above the rest
Of human sadness and depression. Yet
Of course that did not end well

Soon we «broke up»
It was October 21, I was 13 and something
Maybe a couple of more adult thoughts
My first big scar, my first and biggest disappointment
In people and especially in myself
You know, he bullied me, not in my face of course
But left some insecurities for me
And for my future decades, for my future men
At the age of 13 I had to deal with that, you know

And now I think that was the moment
When my biggest dream became dull
Became dusty, broken and forgotten
Because I wasn't such a special girl
Because I wouldn't find love for many
Years more and many more mistakes
And many scars, and burns and broken bones
Many more. And each would left a band
White stripe with drips of blood and tears
Although instead of blood I would completely
Lose my dreams.

17. ***

Have you ever asked yourself what is
The one thing you would not be able to live without
The thing nothing would be the same without

Is it the air stuck forever in your lungs?
Is it the viviparous drops of water on your forehead?
Maybe
But
Maybe not?

For me it is something different, something we barely ever lived
    without
Something more vivid than any of your tired ideas and dreams
If you have them, of course
If I have them too

Language. My Language. Language of our ancestors, of our future
    generations
Of my future children after all
Every sound I make, every breath accompanied with thoughts
Do you know how to think without words?
Maybe animals do, or maybe they have their own Language
Their own ways of expressing their lives, themselves after all
What if we do too

Language changed us forever and taught us to believe in things
In God, in death, in chaos
Maybe not in order

But even though Language simplifies us
It makes us more complex at the same time
Because we learned to distinguish our emotions
Our lives one from another

It is a simplified word in complex souls
Or a very complex soul in a very simple world

What is it for you?

18. The idea of Order at Villars-sur-Ollon

Every season the village seemed to become a new place
In summer cows' mooing was raising above me together with the
    chorus of their bells
And grass was murmuring that sun and warmth would both last
forever
Every summer was hopelessly endless back then
And every sudden creak of an opening wooden door reminded me
    that I was not alone
Even small places are crowded with life

Every winter the cows stayed silent in their stables
And their bells were taken off and hidden among other things
    waiting to be needed again
This waiting was only interrupted by wind, snow, fog and some-
    times hail
They were playing my soul like a piano, making me nostalgic and
    comfortable
With my duvet in the always vivid and chaotic boarding house
Back then

Every spring was like a rest from reality
I was feeling summer stepping on my toes and trying to break the
    silence of blossoming nature
My dreams were bright and quiet, my days were fullfull with hope
    and faith
Playing with each other in the never-ending dance of routine
But my heart was waiting for a change which would never happen
A change of plans, sudden event, sudden falling in love or a
    sudden break up
Which would never happen
Back then

And autumn brought me together with my age,
Made me a little less of a child, not particularly older to notice
Year by year
My teachers were holding their hands tight always fighting with
    our reckless youth
And these things never changed and never would
Everything was ordered
Back then

When I found out I was living my life in order
I left
Back then

19. What else could I possibly think of

We were all doomed I thought
But of course it was not exactly right
The nature around bloomed
But I forgot it even mattered
I believed the world would broom us away
Outdoors

Maybe that's how depression starts
You start thinking you're a tool and
You will be used and thrown out
As simple as it is
I thought

The world seemed to me like a huge swimming pool
Where the level of water was too low to swim
But too high to dry out completely
It was dirty and there were lots of dead corpses
Of flies.

My reality at that time was literally a piece of wool
Turfed out from the city streets by the angry wind of fate
and beliefs
We were all about to die soon
I thought
Our bodies would be hidden in a huge communal tomb
Together with our depressive thoughts
I thought

And then I woke up

20. We buried Her in the forest by my house

My dog used to hate only one thing in her life
A tree. It was very lean and lonely
But it had a very unpleasant look
As if it was going to devour your dreams as soon as you
    touched it
And of course as soon as you did
Neither nothing would change in its look
Nor it would stop being lonely
But I really doubt about any of the dreams disappearing

Instead of my dreams
My dog disappeared
I mean not literally, her body was still there
But her consciousness disappeared with her childish dreams
And I never saw any of them

And for four years I believed it happened because I touched
    the tree
But when my little brother committed this crime
Nothing really happened
So maybe my dog's death was my fault, not the tree's
And she died because I believed that my dreams would
Disappear
I didn't consider only one fact

Her name was Dream

21. ***

The Storm
is knocking at my door
I think I am locked
between two sides of the glass in my window
Like a butterfly

I tear myself naked from the chrysalis-like skin
The knocking makes me
Deaf
It is the same gunshot sounds you hear when a police officer
    comes at your door
with a face of an angry grisly

I thought it was funny once

And now I am the prisoner of the storm
Maybe it is weird that a big girl like me is still scared of it
But like an executor sees death in the eyes of a criminal
I see my misery through the water

The sky must be crying

And still I am alone in this little house
It seems huge now that I can't get out of it
Can't I?
I could try
But I would still be alone and it would be worse
Being alone in a little house is better than in the

Whole world

22. ***

Bulky. Buried under the rat sky
full of tailed sun-rays.
One soulless bite of concrete.

The smell of urine and damp walls
chases our quiet neighbors.
Who are we to judge the imperfection anyway
?
The benches in front of each porch,
cigarette butts and beer bottles under the windows–
these make the picture complete,
nostalgic even.

It was covering us with dark shade–
many short years ago,
us, hiding from our omniscient mothers.
And each knew…
If we went home to drink water
we would not go out until the next day.
And it didn't seem funny

I wonder… are these the memories
that make my childhood so precious and so distant

23. When I stare in the mirror sometimes I see Her staring back with these water drops eyes and little Mona Lisa smile. I wonder if that's too much to be an individual and not enough to be a person.

I wonder if that's how other people see themselves, reflected in this almost ideal surface, not alive.

And I also wonder why I always see Her and not me. I never believed when He said She reminded of me so much.

Maybe that is exactly the false reason of Him saying "we" need to take a pause.

A pause from reality I ask Him. He never answers.

When we first met after 3 years long marathon of love, candles which smelled too sweet but I never complained, of kisses that used to leave wet spots on my cheeks, of beautiful but fake words that He used to love as much as my parents hated Him, I couldn't make myself say anything. I stared at His grave and didn't say a word. I didn't cry even when I saw Her grave for the first time.

I only cried when I realized there was no space left for me. No place for my grave.

24. Post mortem

It looks at me with 3
Black Eyes.
I feel more than dead and more than alive.
I am more free and I am a slave
of my own choice, my last wish.
I can go away, but I won't, will I?
Because I chose NOT TO BE instead of
TO BE.
That is not a question for me.

Dulce periculum is long gone now,
And what's left is to go ad meliora.
This fancy dusty words make me feel heroic.
And I am ready to follow the steps of The Paradise Lost
To find my little lost paradise.
With no apples.

I have no motive to take my own life,
But it feels sweet to think that I am more mad than the others.
Madness is some kind of a sinful desire, if you chose to be mad.

And so I eat my 2 eyes and leave the third one.
It's for dramatic effect, it's the final act of my tragedy.
So take me, my deadly nightshade,
My fruitful Belladonna.

25. ***

Heartless

She smiles. Even when she cries.
She says she has to be strong.
She says she's happy, but she lies.
She's lost in people. She's wrong.

This "she" became her name now,
This "she" is a picture of her.
But there's no soul. You ask me how.
It's dead. A fox with no fur.

Color

This all is more of a portrait
It doesn't seem to be real
I could've given her a trait
And it would probably heal
"It". I don't want to say "her".
I could've given "it" a cœur.

But I didn't, because she's in black
And in white. A very old picture.
I didn't mean for lack
Of balance, capacity. Mixture
Of obscure lines is sketched
On a wall with a little warm coal.
And even this wall's been patched.
Even it lives with no goal.

Nails

Maybe she was a cat.
And this is one of her lives.
The 10th. 11th–a rat.
But now she's stuck, so she dives
Lower and lower. Enough?
The pressure will ruin her ribs.
It's ok. This is a tough
Passage through all of her fibs.

And maybe even before
She'll eat both of her lungs,
Scratched with claws. And what for?
To breathe in the ocean.

Done.

26. ***

The screen of my laptop became not black
And maybe not white, but still in between
My heart wants to smoke, there's only one pack
One cigarette left, where're my nineteen

In my little soul there's spilled gasoline
One cruel spark, one tiny emotion
Will set on fire their last heroine
Left neuron cells will kneel in devotion

I'm left forgotten in foolish notion
Of my own night becoming the day
When moon becomes sun in endless motion
The sky of my thoughts turns out to be grey

Who am I among my own questions
I try to gather my teared sections

27. ***

Ink curls add up in crooked words,
The meaning stays untouched,
Mistaken even, read all wrong.
It might take long, long time

Until her mind will collect
Uneven thoughts with blank design
And write a strict and cold one word,
One letter maybe, one big knot .

And when she's left and left the white,
All white with little stripes of black,
We from above can only see the title of
Unnamed thing. Unnamed letter, nameless sigh.

The title says: "From US Force"
And something else, but we can't see
And I suppose somebody's son or
Husband's buried, lost or gone...

And all in white, among the black
The lost one can't be found soon.

28. Arabica

The coffee's hot in white ceramic cup,
Its steam curls up my hands, my arms. The weather
outside is full of sun, but fools me up.
I hear the wind and coolness. Secret blether
Of their creaky voices shuts my mind.
I hear same sounds right inside of me.
I wonder if I have been also blind
Like you. My coffee can't be tea.

29. Medical education

Once I was asked a very interesting question during my biology
    class
My friend asked me what I thought people were made of
Only now I understand what he actually meant by that
Because in fact
We are not made of flesh and bones
Of ligaments and blood vessels

We are made of barbed wire and thin glass
We are able to see each other so clearly and so neatly
But never able to get over the wall without cutting our soft hearts

We are made of swear words and night stands
Trying to break through our daily routine
Trying to break the rules making ourselves feel alive

We are made of fake gold rings from the suspicious-looking shops
    in the center of Moscow
From headphones tied in a knot
Inventing love and feelings
When in fact we are slowly dying trying to drag somebody else
    with us

We are made of dyed screaming-pink hair with split ends
To feel special, to feel noticed, to feel excluded
From coca-cola. From sprite. From fanta and mirinda
To feel our empty souls with bubbling feeling of neverEEeending
    anxiety
To fill ourselves with something

And what do you think we are made of
I asked him then

And he said
I don't think you are right, Jessie
I think we are made of nothing

30. Nursery house

When my husband was in prison
Well he still is in prison, but not my husband anymore
I thought it would be like in those beautiful films with hap-
     py endings
Because I thought I loved him

I came to see him five times
And although I could come more often than that
I didn't want to
It really takes a couple of lives to learn seeing your own life
     going nowhere

Every time he told me he would be out soon
And everything I had to do was wait
But it is never that easy is it
And apart from waiting
I had to look in the mirror every day realizing
That I did't eat enough, did't sleep enough, did't go out,
     did't see my friends or my family
That I did't actually live
I was waiting

I've never seen a single person
For whom waiting did any good
It certainly did not for me

I was sitting on my bed
Every morning
And every evening

Counting seconds
Counting moments
Counting happy days
And when I reached nine
I always had to stop
And I didn't know whether it was nine seconds, nine weeks
    or nine years
It was as if I suddenly was nine years old
Not knowing exactly what to do with my life
With my own future

I have to admit this feeling was very nostalgic
But it was also tiring, I was ageing very very slowly
It felt like my husband was around 60 years old
And I was still becoming younger

At first when I told him I couldn't do it anymore
I didn't feel anything
But when another couple of years passed by
I found myself crying into the pillow
Because it did not help me
I was a newborn baby
And I needed somebody to take care of me
Since I couldn't do it myself

31. **Drip Drip**

Why, rain, do you hit me hard?
My sorrow didn't ask for it.
Your drops can leave your business card
instead of slashes full of peat.

Why is your water dipped in scorn?
Each oblique stroke–improper wrath,
a proper fraction's ruined, torn,
where every second means one fourth.

Why does your lightning seem so loud
when its whisper cuts my eyes?
And every tear is a scout,
slides down the eaves with butterflies.

Come, silly rain, in my soul
and wash my veins with your blood.
Don't leave a single dirty mole,
Take off my heavy layer of mud.

32. Russia somnos mittantur in corde meo

Sleeping in hearts of snow-white men,
Who froze forever in taunting blizzard,
Great Bear is torpid, the sky is it's den,
The northern wind is called "The White Wizard."
Let the snow of this country shelter the corps,
Hide their navy-blue flame of eyes.
The book of their freedom still quietly warps
From having been held over the lies.
My fingers can't move, my limbs are shaking,
I hear the roaring rattle of rifles.
Ay, fatherland, you are still coarsely raking
Down this game written in cyphers.
One day our Lent will come to its end,
And maybe we'll soak the blood off the ground.
We are like children who were rent
From their mothers' arms. Our cry... was it loud?

About the Author

Anna Schmalinsky (real surname Emelianova) was born in 2003 in Tyumen, in Western Siberia. As a creative pen name she chose her great-grandmother's surname – in her memory. Despite her young age, she has already received several awards. Her works were published in numerous magazines, in Russia as well as in Finland, Germany, Canada and Israel.

She has been writing poetry in Russian since she was 14, in English – since she was 16.

In 2020 her book of Russian poems, *Moy mir raskrashen v rovnuyu polosku* (My world is even-striped) was published in Krasnoyarsk. She also actively works in the genre of video poetry. Currently she resides in the UK and is a student at d'Overbroeck's School in Oxford.

Lightning Source UK Ltd.
Milton Keynes UK
UKHW052248301220
375860UK00009B/356